Lamps and Lampshade Making

-Including the Pedestal Table Lamp, Pendant Ceiling Light, Bracket Wall Fixture, Portable Floor Lamp, and Fifty Lamps and Shades-

By

S. Palestrant

British Library Cataloguing-in-Publication Data
A catalogue record for this book is available from
the British Library

Lamps and Lampshades

𝒯able 𝒫edestal ℒamp

LAMPSHADE

Plastic material comes in many forms—in solid sheets, bars, rods, etc., in films, and in various degrees of viscosity as liquids. Such liquids can span open areas up to twenty square inches. Framing members made of wire should be constructed and dipped into this viscous material. Its cohesive quality causes this material to fasten itself firmly over the structural outline while the surface tension of the material itself causes it to span the intervening openings as a tightly-drawn film. Upon drying through evaporation, this film becomes a strong, firm material, having the strength and rigidity of cellophane—when increased in thickness, it will become stronger. The lampshade herein detailed is intended to fit the pedestal lamp base previously described.

The top and bottom squares are made of 3/8″ x 3/32″ semi-hard flat brass stock. In order to get a sharp right angle bend, cut halfway through the inside flat before bending. Tap lightly and evenly to prevent fracturing the material. File a mitred joint where the two ends meet and braze or sweat-solder the junction.

Join both these metal square loops with a 9½″ #8 semi-hard brass wire. Braze or solder them to the appropriate inside corners of each loop. Add another such wire rib amidship of each side of the top and bottom loops. One inch to the left and one to the right of each of these midribs, solder a wire that is bent to cross the top and follow back as an adjoining rib of the next side of the shade, see diagram. Covering the top corner areas, solder an 8″ square of copper mesh mosquito wire. When dipped, this will give the effect of a sparkle surface plastic insert.

Attach the 4½″ disc so that it joins up all the intersecting ribs that appear across the top of the shade. Add a 1″ brass washer over the center of this plate and drill the hole through. Polish and buff all the metal parts so that they will remain bright under the protective coating of the liquid plastic material.

Now the shade is immersed into a vat of viscous plastic span liquid and tilted so that the excess resin will run off to leave an even film. This viscous material spans all surface between the metal ribs just as soap film would form when a child's bubble-making loop is immersed into lathered water. Allow it to harden and you will find that it results in a clear, transparent, firm film of sufficient strength to make its handling reasonably safe. A harder and heavier film can be achieved by spraying or redipping the shade with overcoat sealing plastics.

Dyes and opaque paints may be procured to paint the inside of the various areas with appropriate colors. Plastic pigments are those which will give a wide variety of effects such as a crystal texture, a phosphorescence, a pearl iridescence, etc. Plan the color scheme of the shade to suit the needs of the room and the unit upon which it will be placed, then follow it carefully. This will reduce error to a minimum for it is practically impossible to remove the paint once applied. When this is done and the paint is dried sufficiently, a fixing medium is sprayed to render the colors permanent.

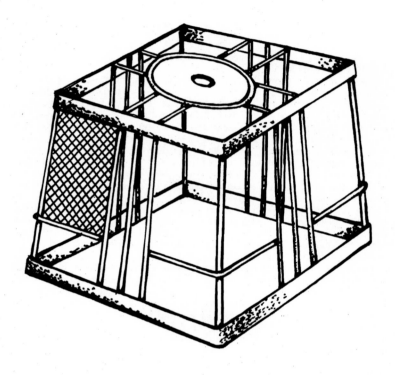

BASE

Lamp bases are a more constant factor than the lampshade. Shades may be recovered, altered or replaced, but the base invariably remains. It is only when major redecorative surgery is applied to the room, or when a complete change of scheme is involved that lamp bases are replaced.

These stands have been made of many materials; wood, metal, ceramic, stone, glass, etc., so why not of plastic material. Belt buckle cast or extruded stock is used. In this case it is brown, square, smooth-surfaced, combined with round, fluted ivory colored plastic material. To avoid the monotony of texture, a decorative square base is purchased for it at any electrical supply house. These plastic buckle bars are cut to sizes indicated in the stock bill. These parts now constitute the major height of the pedestal base.

Assemble all parts in the order shown in the diagram starting with the lock nut under the metal base which threads on the electrical pipe up to the lamp socket set within the harp. Attach the double twisted strand lamp cord to the binding posts of this socket and lead it through the center of the electrical pipe, then out from the lead-hole in the base. End this extension wire with a male plug. Do this before you screw all parts firmly together.

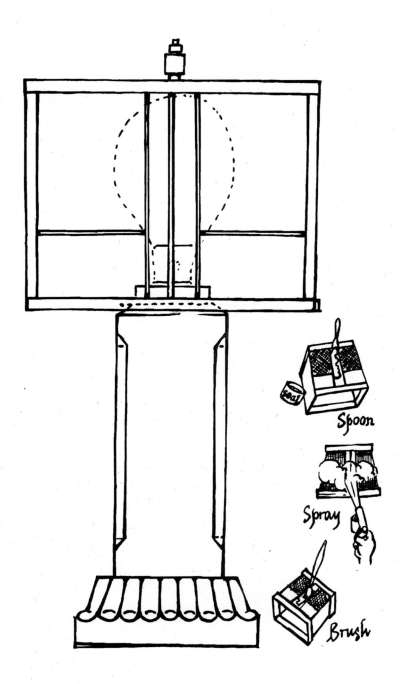

Spoon

Spray

Brush

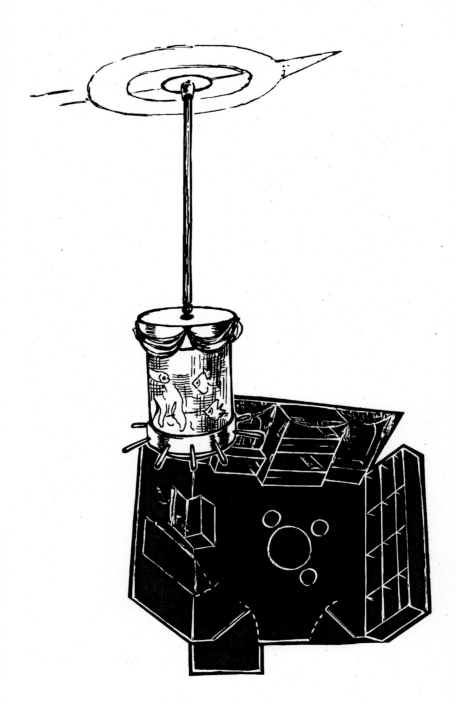

Pendant Ceiling Light

Let us suppose we need a ceiling light for a child's room. Within this room we have the following influences which might affect the final form of this lamp. It is a boy's room, a boy about 10 or 12 years of age. This boy's preference runs towards ships and things nautical. The room, about twelve feet square, has a ten foot ceiling. It contains a double bunker bed with pin-up binnacle lights along each forward poster. This bed is set between two high windows. Sea-chest window-seats are beneath them and a valance of heavy fishing net hangs across the room above these windows and the topmost posts of the bunker beds.

The wall next to it has 6 foot shelves stretching in an unbroken line across the room. These are topped with models of sea-going vehicles.

The wall opposite this is broken by a door leading into the bathroom and flanked by a Governor Winthrop drop-leaf desk. This is fronted by a Windsor or rush-seated, ladder-back chair. Above the desk hangs a large treasure map with a parchmented wall bracket light fastened along either side of it.

The fourth wall contains the entrance door balanced by the closet door on its right. Between them may be a bracket console with a mirror above it. Directly in the center of the room is a three or four foot circular pedestal table with three or four chairs straddling it. It is above this table that the ceiling outlet appears from which a fixture should extend.

Three ideas immediately suggest themselves. They are: 1) a recessed circular fixture to resemble a porthole with its swing door; 2) a circular flush fixture which may be made to look like a ship's compass; 3) a pendant fixture extending four feet below the ceiling level to show a main theme of a ship's steering wheel. Let the latter one be that which we will develop. These are the reasons:

We need a great deal of general, diffused illumination within the room. This is more easily accomplished by suspending a "boom" light to a position somewhere within the volume of the room than by means of a lamp set high. Greater efficiency is possible. We can also arrange to cast direct light directly upon this circular table through an opening in the bottom of the lamp. This may be magnified with a Fresne lens inserted to form a spotlight. The open area at the top of this fixture makes it possible to spill a good deal of the otherwise wasted direction of the beams upon the ceiling area. This will add to the diffused illumination of a general nature. The sides of this pendant fixture may be made of translucent material which can permit as much light through as you'd care to allow. This can be controlled to create color notes which may build up the atmosphere and mood of the room towards its logical goal. In all, this pendant lamp serves a triple purpose. It sets up diffused general lighting to permit the unhampered activity of the room; it supplies direct lighting over the prescribed area of operation and aids the decorative and illusionary nature of the entire room design. Therefore, we chose this lamp.

Bracket Wall Fixture

This lamp is an improvement over the turn-of-the-century gas jets in both appearance and efficiency. Though it has taken on unprecedented forms through modern design and engineering, even become part of the architectural structure rather than the adopted piece of ornamental wall trim, it remains to a great extent, an accepted necessity in most small homes of traditional design. Suppose we seek a wall lamp fixture which will suit the needs of an 18th Century American dining room. A pair of these lamps are suggested to flank the buffet sideboard, to lend the proper air and some authenticity. Neither the furniture nor the furnishings are of early colonial or provincial style. It therefore rates elegance. Since the buffet sideboard suggests dining and serving, what is more appropriate than to convert a platter and a cup and saucer into lamp to identify its place in the room. One might use an extra matching piece of the household service china. However, it is not out of place to choose an individual piece.

These brackets can be made of identical platters and identical cups and saucers, but it is still within good taste—in fact it would prove an interesting variation, to use mated pieces. They may be identical in shape and vary in decoration or vary in shape though similar in decoration. Any of these combinations, if selected in close harmony, should be recognized as a "mated pair."

Drill a hole through the center of the plate, the saucer and the bottom of the cup. Use a triangular file ground to a 45 degree angle point in a hand brace while the point of this home made bit is bathed in a sludge made of emery dust in kerosene and walled in by a clay bank. Slow, careful grinding will lap-grind a hole through. Avoid using excess pressure on the brace. It will crack or break the delicate chinaware.

Bend a piece of electrical pipe threaded on both ends, one end to a "U" curve with a six inch diameter, and the other end to a 90 degree curve in the opposite direction. Attach the 90 degree bend to the large plate using a screw cap in front and fixing it firmly with a wide washer and double nut from behind. Place felt washers between the metal parts and the china surface to prevent it from cracking or grinding through later.

Set the saucer on the end of the "U" curve with a metal plate cap beneath and the cup on top. Separate all parts with felt pads. Thread these together firmly. Screw a bridge socket on to the protruding pipe nipple in the cup. Thread a #18 lamp cord through the curved electrical pipe and screw one end to the binding posts of the lamp socket. Slip the candle collar in place and screw in a small flame lamp. If a lead-in is exposed in the wall, then tie in a short wire to it leading from this newly made lamp. Tape the terminals properly and hang up the plate bracket lamp to hide the lead-in. If no such feed wire is available, attach a wall socket plug to the extension wire, first checking to see that the wire is long enough to reach the nearest outlet.

Use a three wire "finger-grip" which grips the plate rim as a means of hanging this bracket lamp to the wall. There are several such available in the market or at your local hardware, electrical or decorator's shop.

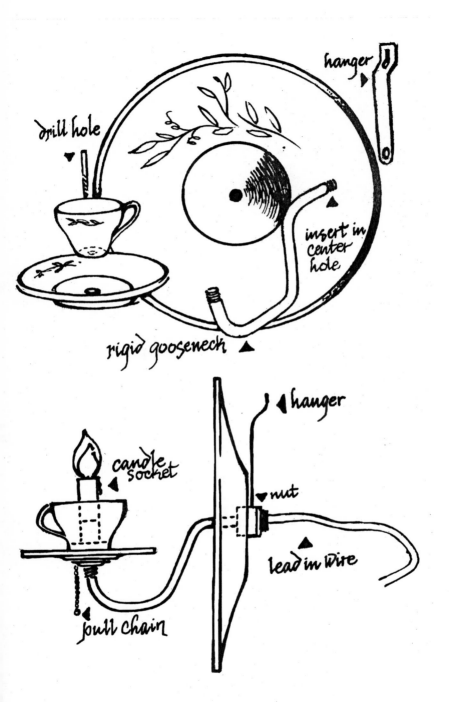

hanger

drill hole

insert in
center
hole

rigid gooseneck ▲

hanger

candle
socket

nut

lead in wire

pull chain

Portable Floor Lamp

As we consider the portable group—the floor lamp in particular—we should review a few thoughts about the principles of lighting. It is necessary that no glare exist in the room. To permit this is to give eye fatigue, consequently followed by general body tiredness, our official sanction. This is not to be. Glare, therefore, whether directly from the lamp or coming indirectly from some glossy wall or bouncing off a picture glass, is to be carefully avoided. Secondly, since man has developed his ability to live by his sight, he has been accommodating his vision to reflected light from below his eye level and shading or diffusing his original source from overhead. Witness the need of the protective hair-dos of such groups as the Seminole Indians and the head gear developed by farmers, out-of-door workers and soldiers. All of this tends to prove the biologic need for this adjustment. Hence, portable lamps should not be too high, should cast the major portion of their illumination downward and should be shielded from thrusting light directly into the eyes of the person no matter what his position should be in relation to that lamp.

Further eye consideration is that its structure is intended to adjust itself to changing intensities. If we study the out-of-doors where man originally funcioned and developed, we would find that overall changes in light were never radical. It ran the gamut from bright daylight to stygian darkness, but this never happened with any great degree of suddenness. This should show us that general room illumination should not run to extremes in intensity and that changes between rooms or even general areas in the room should not be too strongly opposed in the scale.

Furthermore, at any time during the day or night out-of-doors, the normal difference of illumination between the highlight and the shadow of an area is not extreme. To all this the eye has been developed to make its adjustment. It follows, therefore, that general or key light of a room should not be extreme in either direction. This will bring on early fatigue, whether we wish it or not. Once the proper key light is set, the specific lighting such as supplied by a floor or table lamp must create highlights and shadows but not too far up and down the scale beyond the general illumination of the room. About a thirty per cent variation is adequate—then toward the highlights and about twenty into the shadow area. The eye can stand more of the shadow because it does not excite or stimulate the optic nerve. So, avoid constant general light without shading it to avoid fatigue and create shadows through the correlated highlights to provide resting areas for the observer.

Color is another factor in this review because it's been proved that stimulation can be increased with the use of certain hues, intensities and combinations (juxtapositioning). Likewise restfulness and seditation can be controlled. Selection of color, therefore, must be based upon the kind of room, its size, its function and the specific purpose of a particular area.

50 Lamps and Shades

CHAIR-LEG—LAMP with MICA SHADE

Odd pieces of spindle turnings like those of chair and table legs may easily be converted to end-table lamps. Turn an ample base plate to be used under this spindle piece then drill through the center of both. Insert a pipe to hold the parts firmly together and set a lamp socket on top. Embed the bottom holding screw into the base to avoid lamp rocking and table scratching. The body piece may be given a metallic finish, even "antiqued", painted or wood finished if the natural grain permits. In the former case, the lampshade could be covered with metallic cloth and edges bound by tape having metal rings threaded over it.

WALL-LAMP SCREEN

Bend a length of baling wire to the shape of the frame shown. Form the side panels gently tapering the ends to fit smoothly along the side pieces of the center panel. Solder these firmly together. Thread the extending arms of the screen through clamp-jaw plates made of medium gauge tin-plate. Solder these in place to keep them from twisting. Wrap a sheet-metal clip over these crossed arms. Pinch it close, then secure it firmly with soft solder. Paint it in gay colors. Add ribbed or smooth translucent plastic panels to fill the open areas. Drill holes around the edges by which it may be to the frame with plastic lace.

SOLID SHADE

Mark off and cut two pieces of $\frac{1}{8}$ cork. Each should fit half-way around a truncated, circular, wire lamp shade frame. Bind the cork covering to the top and bottom shade loops with a like-hued pas partout tape. Where the ends of these cork pieces touch each other, lash them together with wide Florentine leather lace. Cross-thread it through the holes punched in correct position. Spray tempera paint over patterned stencils, cut-outs or template masks to get a bottom border design. Protect the paint, lace, cork and tape with a film of plastic spray. Additional coats may be added if necessary.

RAW-EDGED PANEL SHADE

Cut four rectangular sides out of $\frac{1}{8}$" mahogany plywood, each measuring 12 x 9" and the top panel one foot square. Drill a series of holes parallel to the edges of these panels except at the bottom. No holes are drilled there. Twist a double strand of soft thin (28 gauge) copper wire into not too tight a spiral. Anneal the wire to soften it again. Finish the panels in a very high gloss finish before assembling them. Drill a $\frac{1}{4}$" hole on center of the one-foot panel. Cement a wide $\frac{1}{4}$" washer to the underside. Lash the panels to each other by threading a spiraling wire through the matching holes with an "over-cast stitch". Twist the ends into a tight roll close to the end hole at the underside of the panels. Spray or brush this copper "lace" with clear lacquer to retain its high polish.

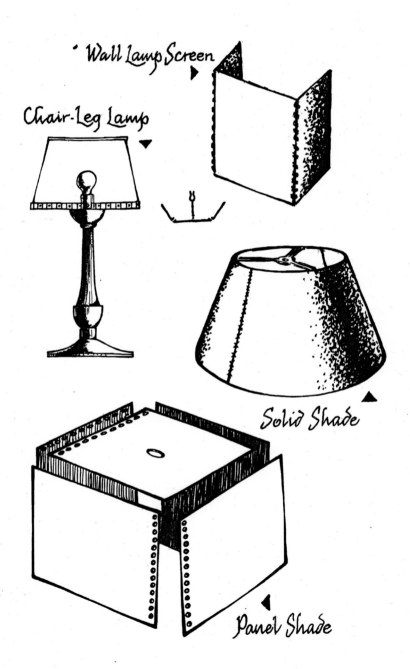

Wall Lamp Screen ▶

Chair-Leg Lamp ▶

Solid Shade ▶

Panel Shade ◀

11

APRON-DRAPED SHADE

Color and polish a plywood disc of desired size. Attach a soft, fine, wire mesh or a plastic net-weave cloth to its edge as a skirt. Gather the material as close as possible to give it the grace of fullness. Cover the joint with an ornamental tape or plastic molding trim. Bind the lower edge with tape or make a fold-over hem to avoid a raw "finish." Fasten the shade to the lamp harp at its screw post to secure it.

RIBBED PLASTIC SHIELD

Heat and form a piece of opal, ribbed, thermoplastic material to curve around the front of a pin-up lamp. Smooth the edges before shaping them. Drill holes to accommodate soft rivets which should be fastened to a metal holding plate. This, in turn, is attached to a pinch clamp used to grip the shield piece to the candle socket of the pin-up lamp. This shield may be clamped on and off quickly and easily.

TOLE CONE

A circular pattern, as shown in the diagram, is cut out of lightweight tinplate and rolled to form a flat cone. Fasten it with a series of flat-beaded rivets in a straight line through the overlapping flap. It may be sweat soldered if preferred. The base lip of the shade may be left raw but smooth, bent back to form a narrow fold or be soldered edge flush to a piece of baling wire. Attach an inner ring and spider near its apex to which a lamp harp can be connected. Paint the lampshade in bright lacquer colors. Pennsylvania Dutch designs are in good taste for this shape of an informal shade. In a more formal vein it might tend toward classical border units like floral, frets or sea inspired motifs.

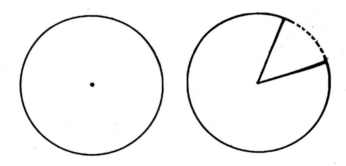

PAPER-DECOUPAGE SHADE

Trace the pattern shape of a lamp frame on a piece of construction paper and cut it out. Punch a set of evenly-spaced holes along both edges, then set the paper "skin" in position on the frame. Hold it in place with strategically-placed spring clothes pins while it is attaching it to the frame. Bind them together with lace made of crepe paper cut into thin strips and twisted to resemble string. Join the overlapping edges of the paper covering with rubber cement. Do the same with any loose lace ends. Cut out a floral pattern from a selected piece of wallpaper and cement it to the surface of the lamp shade. A protective coating of clear lacquer or plastic spray should keep it safe from injury due to atmospheric changes and hard handling.

Tole Cone

Decoupage ▶

Apron-Draped Shade

Plastic Shield ▶

PLASTIC-COATED SCREENING

This lampshade only needs the top wire-loop although the one at the bottom may help keep it firmer. Cut a rectangular strip of plastic dipped, porchwire screening. Roll one long edge over the top wire loop and cement the raw edge around it. Do the same at the bottom. The wire screening is rigid enough to support its own weight and needs no cross-bracing. The fine mesh acts as a diffusing screen to break up the raw light of the lamp light inside even though it is transparent. Color may be added by painting pre-defined areas with any of the aniline dyes available.

WIRE-LATTICED SHADE

Half inch, square, galvanized chicken wire, cut to sufficient rectangular length should make a sturdy lampshade frame. Cut the wires past the dimension mark just up to the next parallel wire line, leaving a series of wire fingers extending beyond the required size. These are used to wrap around the cross-wire at the edge next to it or around a heavy wire ring serving as a finishing edge. Half inch square, metal clips might be used as an alternative method. A round or rectalinear piece serving as a top plate will help to reinforce it greatly. Weave heavy wool yarn threads in and out of the holes according to a pattern laid out on squared paper. This creates a design on the lampshade resembling a coarse hand-loomed rug.

FRAMED PANEL SHADE

Flat curtain rods cut lengthwise or brass "U" shaped, single track show case molding can be made into panel frames. This is notched and soldered to proper size and shape. Before each panel is sealed an ornamental glass slide must be inserted. These panels may be fastened to each other and to the spider hoop on top before the glass pieces are set in. This might protect them from heat fracture during the soldering process. The metal frame should be properly smoothed, cleaned and painted before using it as the lampshade.

ACCORDION PLEATED SHADE

Crease a long strip of thin but tough construction paper in a series of alternate and parallel folds. The raw edges may be doubled back and pasted down or straddled with half inch wide pas partout tape, for reinforcement. Punch matching and aligned holes through the vertical center of each folded panel and about two inches from each end. Thread a decorative braid or cord through each set of these holes. By drawing them tightly or not the diameter size of the shade at that point may be regulated to suit the spider hoop which it covers. In that way the general form of the shade can be controlled. Fasten it to the supporting wire rings with tape or lash string.

SWIVEL-LOUVRED SHADE

This lampshade is made of a series of parallel plastic fins. One side of each one is wrapped around a thick aluminum wire and cemented. These louvres are held in place by two, one-half-inch rings of 10 gauge aluminum. One is on top, the other at the bottom of these end-pivoting pieces. The wire pins extending out of each end of these rings are inserted into matched holes drilled through these aluminum rings. Two long wires are anchored in special holes in the bottom ring, extend up vertically through aligned holes in the top ring, bends at right angles across the top of the shade and return on the diametrically opposite side in reverse order. The spider wires cross at right angles on center on top and form a flat loop. This is used to attach the lampshade to the harp.

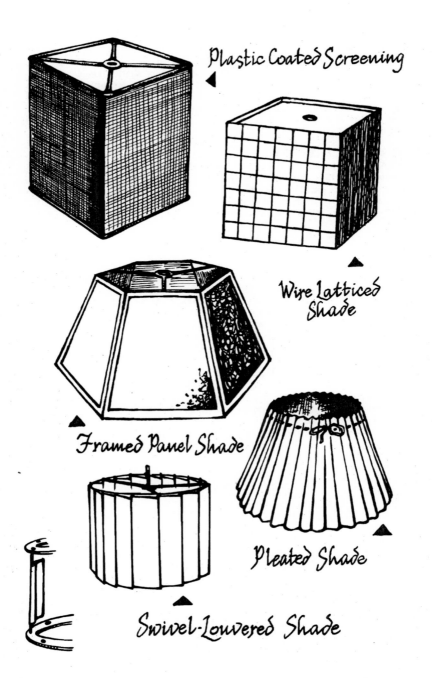

Plastic Coated Screening

Wire Latticed
Shade

Framed Panel Shade

Pleated Shade

Swivel-Louvered Shade

15

RAFFIA-WRAPPED SHADE

Raffia, any other yarn-like material should serve as well, may be wrapped around the wire "arms" of the lamp shade frame in many arrangements to result in a variety of designs. In wrapping the raffia material, it will have to be joined at the ends to lengthen it for continued use. When completed, some kind of protective coating should be used to cover this highly vulnerable material—vulnerable to dirt, moisture and destruction.

BAMBOO SPLINT SHADE

A series of bamboo splint, drilled at both ends are lashed to top and bottom rims of a lampshade frame with plastic tie string or fishing line. Set the splints parallel to each other and overlapping slightly. This shields the light more effectively. The natural finish of bamboo is highly desirable though it may be stained or dip-dyed to match the color scheme of the room.

LATTICED-TOP SHINGLE SHADE

Two sets of long one inch wide strips of flexible plastic material (.050 thick) are set crossing each other in units of 8, 10, or 12 depending upon the desired size of the shape. A square is fashioned in basket-weave ending by wrapping around the top of the wire frame of a square lampshade. The ends are cemented down firmly. Starting at the bottom of the shade wind rows over row of the same strips so that the one above overlaps the strip directly below it for about an eighth of an inch. These wrappings are individual rings whose ends are firmly cemented at one of the corners. The entire construction resembles the siding of a frame house.

NEON BOUDOIR LAMP

The base of this lamp contains the rectifying mechanism needed for neon wiring. The light switch is connected at that point. The neon tubing travels up the pedestal of large ribbed glass tube in which it will glow and cause the lampstand to be illuminated. Of the two extending neon lead tubes, one will travel straight up, bend out at right angles then curl down in an increasing spiral following the walls of an imaginary drum-shaped lampshade. The bottom end of this connects with the other lead tube, making a complete circuit. A hood of the same shape and made of either very finely meshed aluminum wire screening or of flexible plastic sheeting, plain or figured, is set over it to help diffuse the raw quality of this light. This lamp has a low efficiency point.

PLASTIC-CARVED FLUORESCENT LAMP

Cut two, one-inch pieces of Lucite to the indicated shape and polish all surfaces except the edges. Carve an intaglio design on the inside surface of the front section. Use a hand-grinder in much the same manner as a dentist would. Clamp the two halves together with the gray-carved design between them. Set "U" shaped aluminum channels over each edge of these joined pieces of plastic and fasten them with plastic drive screws. Fit the ballast and switch into the hollowed base section, threading the lead wire up one aluminum channel. A short fluorescent lamp is fixed to the top of this Lucite lamp back. Fashion an aluminum shade having two tool clips riveted to the inside of it. These will snap on to the fluorescent tube to shield the eyes from direct light and support the shade. The entire lamp will glow when lit up.

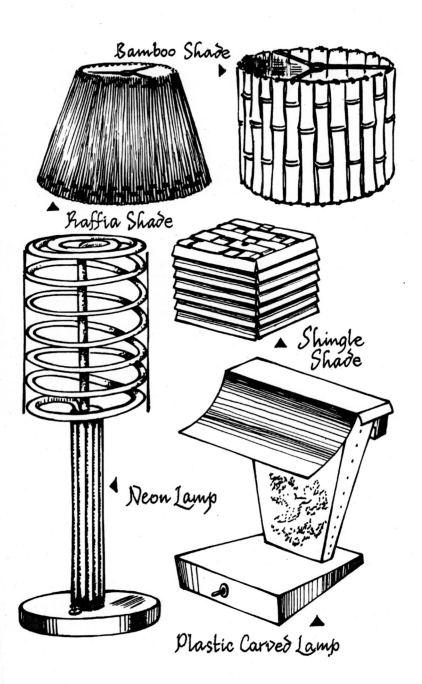

Bamboo Shade

Raffia Shade

Shingle Shade

Neon Lamp

Plastic Carved Lamp

FLEXIBLE, INDIRECT SPOT—TABLE REFLECTOR

A short parabolic reflector bowl is fastened to a hard spring flexible gooseneck. The base is a domed fixture cap mounted on a large weighted automobile hub cap. This is connected to the gooseneck. A ring made of half-inch "L" beam is riveted to three rigid wire legs ending in a socket collar clamp. The ring is drilled and tapped for thumb control set-screws to hold an encased Fresne lens. If the metal is match it may be buffed to a high gloss. If not, paint it with a contrasting crackle paint over an undercoat of colored lacquer. Wire it with a base switch. The lamp serves as an indirect light and for special needs as a spot light.

CANOPY PEDESTAL LAMP

A serrated glass tube of reasonable diameter is mounted on a small, inverted cut-glass bowl or square sided dish with a hole drilled through its center. Hold these together with a length of electrical pipe and capped at each end, properly protected against breakage. Attach a one-lamp socket and harp on top and wire it for incandescent lighting. Make the "canopy shade" of any of the many transparent casting resins. Follow, very carefully, the directions given with the plastic compound. Use an appropriately-shaped glass mixing bowl or metal wash basin. After it has been cured drill for the harp screw and anchor it with a glass finial. These, glass and plastic, may be made of tinted material.

MODERN VANITY LAMP

Screw a one and a half inch square, polished brass tubing into the notched corner of a two inch thick polished walnut base about eight inches square. Braze four wire prong supports for the ring which hangs over the lamp. Wire it with a pull chain socket after setting in a walnut plug-cap with a pipe nipple through it to hold the socket in place. Make the shade of walnut veneer cemented on a linen back (U. S. Plywood Corp.). Glue the flap-over edge to make a clean cut joint. Make a grooved reflector-rest attachment to dip low and rest on the lamp ring previously made. Use a thin, soft brass strip to edge the lamp and flap over the top and bottom lampshade rings to help lampshade keep its shape and remain firm.

DRIFTWOOD LAMP

A well-chosen, weather-worn piece of driftwood log can make a very interesting time-sculptured pedestal for a lamp. Drill a hole through its vertical center large enough to accommodate a section of threaded pipe. Have it extend through the base piece (also driftwood) and extend up sufficiently to set a push button socket. A round tapered shade covered with natural colored Monk's cloth should look well with the darker toned driftwood. The lamp body and base may be highlighted with ochre or buff to contrast with the deep brown tones of the crevices. A section of driftwood branch will make a proper looking finial. Wire it and you have a fine ranch house or modern-looking lighting piece.

NEWEL-POST—PEDESTAL LAMP

Bannister newel posts have been turned in many interesting forms and a section of a discarded one can be converted into an unusual pedestal lamp. Saw off as much of the top section as would look well and drill down through its center to accommodate a section of electrical pipe. Extend it and add the necessary fixture to hold an opal glass reflector bowl. Set a silk-covered, wire framed lampshade on it to rest upon the bowl's edge. Attach a base plate large enough to give it sufficient stability, then wire it for incandescent lighting. The silk shade might have another colored lining to create color interest when the lamp is lit.

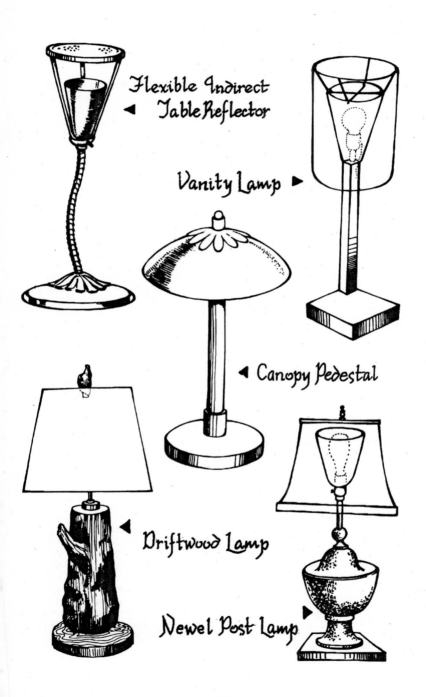

Flexible Indirect
◄ Table Reflector

Vanity Lamp ►

◄ Canopy Pedestal

◄ Driftwood Lamp

Newel Post Lamp ►

BAMBOO LAMP—METAL SHADE

This lamp seeks its realization through the use of lengths of bamboo shoots. A sturdy-sized section should serve as the pedestal piece with a wood plug in each end holding the electrical pipe in position. Greater width for base-stability may be added by lashing to the bottom section with shorter pieces of bamboo with split reeds. These too, may be plugged and so serve as a planter lamp in addition. A bottom piece of wood may be cut to matching silhouette to cap the individual bamboo vessels as one. Wire the lamp with either single socket and harp or a double socket attachment. The lamp shade is cut and fashioned out of a section of fancy radiator metal grill, bordered along the top and bottom rims with template—silhouette strips soldered to it. Polish or lacquer it as desired. Use a small bamboo section as a finial piece.

WROUGHT-IRON—LYRE LAMP

This is an excellent porch lamp though it can be used for other parts of the house, if suitable in style. The body is made of 1 x 2 inch rectangular tubing. The harp form is shaped of $1'' \times \frac{1}{4}''$ strap iron. The "strings" are $\frac{1}{4}''$ rods. The bottom of the strap iron harp is punched through (heated first) and forged open to permit the center tube to ease through it. The string rods are inserted into holes and mushroomed at the ends to hold firmly in place. The upper ends are fastened together by two strips of 1/16-inch sheet metal with rivets spaced to do the job. A cap set on the top of the tube serves to hold a threaded electrical pipe which connects to the dual-socket unit. The bottom place through a hole in the rectangular, chamfered marble base, splayed open then cemented. The shade is shaped in front and back with sides as fill-in panels. This wire frame with a molding grill on top and solid strip on bottom is covered with spun glass. Paint all metal parts.

ROPE-TWIST—WOOD LAMP

Carve or turn a twenty-two inch length by three inches in diameter wooden rope twist. Finish in dark wood color. Cut out a ten inch heavy wooden disc for the base. Finish that in natural light color. Attach a strip of light colored, linen-backed wood veneer (matching the bases) around a ten-inch drum wire lampshade frame. Attach it with dark $\frac{1}{4}$ inch wide rawhide lace with an overcast stitch. Drill or punch holes in the veneer to accommodate the lace. Before assembling the lamp, cut off a two inch section to serve as a finial. Top it with a $1\frac{1}{2}$ inch wooden ball. Screw the base to the pedestal rope, drill for and insert the lamp cord. Use a threaded nipple on top to attach the lamp socket and the harp to the rope. Arrange to have the lead-in wire emerge from the side of the base block. Cement a felt pad under it for scratch-protection.

DECANTER LAMP

A large, Italian wine bottle half covered with reed and raffia dressing is the basis of an interesting novelty lamp. Drill a hole in its bottom and set in a piece of electrical pipe to extend about four inches above its lip. Slide a cork bushing into the bottle mouth to hold the pipe securely upright. Wrap multicolored strips of raffia in continuous vertical windings around a wire lampshade frame. Pack these strands close together allowing no flapping or sagging of each wrapping. Spray a plastic coat or brush it lightly with a thinned solution of white shellac to help protect the shade. Convert one of the Swiss novelty wood-carved corks into a lamp finial to top it off. If the lamp appears top heavy, fill the bottle with beach sand. This will add greater stability. Select a bottle having colored glass, if possible.

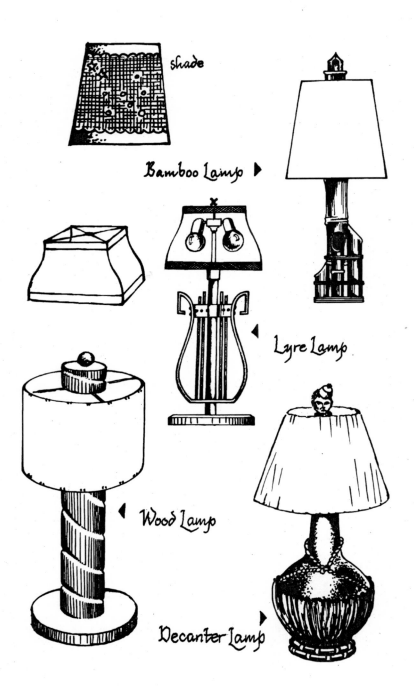

shade

Bamboo Lamp ▶

Lyre Lamp ◀

Wood Lamp ◀

Decanter Lamp ▶

GLASS BRICK—UTILITY LAMP

Make this lamp starting with a large glass brick. Drill holes through the center, top and bottom to accommodate the pipe necessary for wiring. This pipe should be long enough to pass through the wood block base, the glass brick and a metal or wooden cap plate. It is gripped at the bottom with a lock nut set in a counter-bored hole and on top with a coupling nut to permit the addition of the lamp socket section. The lampshade is made of four tapered panels of eighth inch plywood. Decorate each with a pierced design. Join them at the corners with angle irons set inside and fastened with split rivets. The finial which repeats the material of the body of the lamp is made of clear plastics with scored cross lines to simulate the effect of the glass brick. Thread the bottom hole directly or use a screw insert.

CHILD'S PIN-UP LAMP

Several large children's play blocks are used for the body of this lamp. Drill a set of half-inch aligned holes through them. In the center block drill one at right angles to it. Counterbore half way in on the original hole to accommodate an outside pipe barrel bushing with a right angle threaded hole. Link all these together with short threaded pipe sections. Use flange plates on the outside to clamp these blocks together. Use a short extension nipple to set the lamp off the correct distance from the wall plate which is a painted plywood cut-out. Add the lamp socket section to the top. Convert a toy drum of the right size to become the shade. Remove one side and insert the wired washer so that it sets firmly upon the harp screw.

LIBRARY—TABLE LAMP

This lamp is purely an assembly job. All parts are stock pieces available at most every metal drawing and spinning parts company. The size and complication of the lamp depends upon the ability of the craftsman to conceive a unit. The lampshade is built upon a wire frame. The "lamp skin" is cut and mounted. Binding tape is an effective material and does an excellent job in holding the stretched parchment to the lampshade hoops. Cut-out pieces of stained mica are cemented along the top edge. Nail heads decoration gives a wide latitude to an imaginative decoration.

SPIRAL SHIELD—ADJUSTABLE LAMP

The vertical upright pipe, screwed into a heavy, metal base much like that which supports merchandise display stands, becomes the stanchion for the bridge arm. This arm is clamped over the upright allowing it to be moved up or down and fixed at any given position. The lamp socket section is attached to the end of the extending arm with a swivel joint. The shield is made of a pennant-shaped triangular piece of frosted lumarith. This is anchored along the top edge of the plastic to the socket holder causing the spiral and progressive reduction of the size of the shield toward the inside of it.

ADJUSTABLE DESK LAMP

Two 1" x ½" oval brass pipe posts, topped by a square brass cross pipe bar serve as the supports for this adjustable lamp. Four inch long slots by ¼" wide are cut just below the top of these posts to accommodate the threaded nipple and thumb screw catch which supports the "S" curved metal shade. The front end of the nipple ends at a right angle elbow connecting to a keyless lamp socket which holds a long lumiline lamp. The connecting wire leads down the oval post into the underside of the gaily colored wooden base to be connected to the canopy push switch.

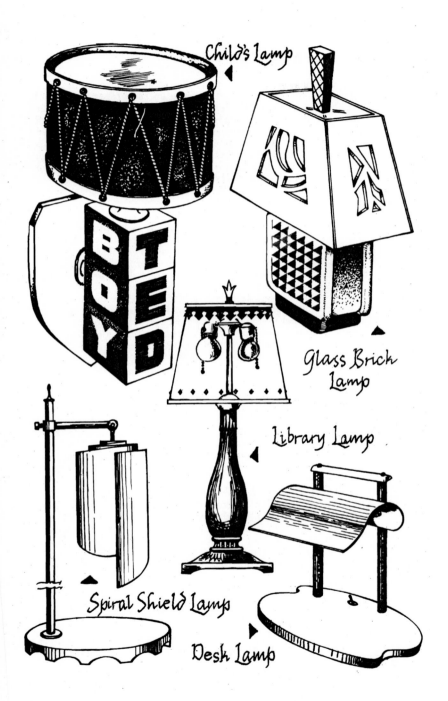

Child's Lamp

Glass Brick Lamp

Library Lamp

Spiral Shield Lamp

Desk Lamp

23

"CHUCKLE-WOOD" LAMP

This "chuckle-wood" material, produced by the U. S. Plywood Corp., is cut into square mounds resembling small pyramids and mounted on a cloth backing. A section of this is cut to make up the proper height and when curled, the correct-sized cylinder. Glue the matching edges from the inside with a tape against the cloth side of the material. Cap each end with a block of wood and clamp the whole thing tightly with a piece of electrical pipe, washer and screw at each end. See that the pipe extends about four inches above to which the lamp socket and harp are screwed. Finish this in any of the popular wood finishes. A simple drum-shaped shade covered with opaque plastic film will look good. A checkered square border design cemented to it along the rim will carry out a repeat of the squared motif of the lamp base itself.

UPHOLSTERED LEATHER LAMP

Around a hollow wooden plinth of a lamp base tack down a padded leather cover with upholsterer's button nails to form an all-over diamond pattern. Finish off the top and bottom by rolling under the raw leather edges and fastening it down in a continued pattern of the button-padded design. The exposed sections of the wood are painted before being upholstered. Natural colored leather with matching buttons against a contrasting-hued paint should go well with a buff-colored lampshade made of coarse-weave, wooly-fibered knubby cloth. The finial is the inverted shape of the base painted to match the leather tones and dotted in diaper design. Use an antiqued brass nail whose head-shape resembles the puffed area of the upholstery created by button identations.

TUBE TWISTED—ROPE LAMP

Three lengths of half or five-eighths inch aluminum or brass tubing (whichever suits the group decoration) are spirally twisted over a tapered sleeve. These are welded to a base plate and cap as shown. Through one of these the lamp cord is drawn starting from a hole in the base plate which opens into the tube and out of a hole in the side of the tube just below the top cap. This, then leads into a pipe nipple screwed into the center hole of the cap ending in the lamp socket within the reflector globe. The lamp shades rests; hangs on the globe edges by its formed wires. Its upper trim is enhanced by the repetition of the round wire open spiral which carries on the motif of the lamp base.

WASH DAY, PIN-UP LAMP

This doll lamp has a half silhouetted wooden and painted figure with pinned arms, one of which pivots and when it does, pulls the lamp's chain switch. The shade is made of bamboo splints lashed to a half wash basket shape and clipped on to the lamp bulb for attachment. The wiring follows through a piece of electrical pipe which is strap-anchored into a half-round dado groove cut along the back spine of the figure. This bends forward on top in a short "S" curve ending with the lamp socket. This enables the lamp bulb to be centered within the shade. Screw a bracket plate on the back and as close to the top of the body as possible to keep it from spinning head downward when hung against the wall.

BEAN POLE ADJUSTABLE FLOOR LAMP

Use a five foot length of polished, square metal tubing for the bean pole body of this floor lamp. Seal the top with a snap-on plate cap and attach the bottom to a galleried, platter-like base piece by brazing it. The lamp shade, a truncated square pyramid is made of coarse cotton shantung

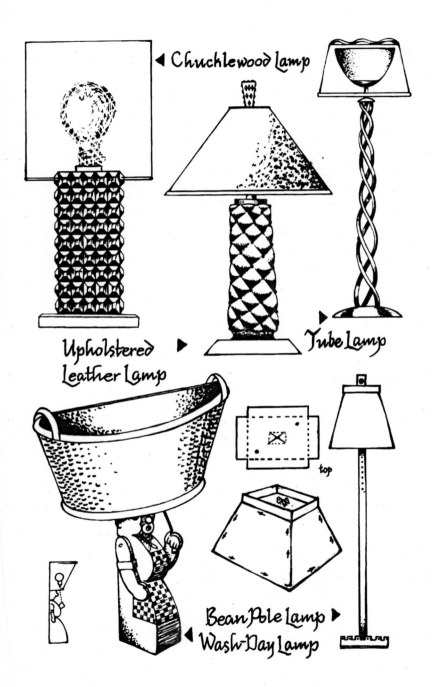

◀ Chucklewood Lamp

Upholstered
Leather Lamp ▶

▶ Tube Lamp

top

Bean Pole Lamp ▶
◀ Wash-Day Lamp

25

material with a large-figured, block-printed lining. This will create a highly decorated lampshade every time the lights are switched on in the lamp and an unadorned one when the lights go off. The lamps themselves are wired to the structure of the shade so that they move with the adjustment of the shade. This holds firmly to the pole by the spring action of the dimples in the flanges matching those made in the pole. The lamp cord extends through the pole and is spring-curled like telephone extensions to open and contract as used.

WROUGHT-IRON BIRD CAGE FLOOR LAMP

A "barrel bird cage" made of three heavy wire hoops and joined by four vertical support rods are, in turn, welded to a ⅝" lamp pipe rack. This is bent into a large circular base to create sufficient stability. The hoops of the "bird cage" may serve as a support for shelves made of heavy gauge, close-meshed screen. The upper end of the pipe rack terminates with the lamp socket and harp on which a wicker-woven, reed shade is supported. The lamp cord extends down through the lamp rack and emerges from an opening at some point of the ring base.

BOWLING GLOBE LAMP

Convert a large bowling or duck pin into a lamp by drilling a hole through its center from top through the bottom. Screw a wooden base plate to it and set in an electrical pipe to hold the lamp cord safely. Attach the lamp socket at the top and a round globe holder to it. Select one which most resembles the size of a bowling ball. If an opaque or heavy translucent glass is unavailable then coat the inside of the globe with oil paint of the chosen color. Get a uniform covering without brush streaks showing by patting the half-wet paint with a cheesecloth pounce ball. Use a pull chain socket switch for convenience.

PLANTER'S LAMP

Secure a fair sized hammered copper flower pot and flat bowl to match. Drill a hole in the bottom of the pot and bolt a brass pipe, threaded on both ends, with a lock nut and washer on each side of the hole. Brace the pipe at the lip-level of the pot with two brass cross wires (11 gauge) which circle the pipe, then are riveted securely in holes at opposite sides of the pot lip. These four braces should be ample. Solder the pot, on center, to the flat bowl with a flat "Z" or "C" foot to raise it about one inch above the bowl bottom. Shape and solder some lengths of galvanized baling wire to form a trellis with two long pricking prongs at its bottom. Paint it to suit. The lampshade is the wire structure covered with colored translucent lumarith. The top hoop has a copper wire wave shaped and soldered to it. Use an exposed copper wire at the bottom too. Wire it, set your plant in order then fill the bowl with an assortment of colored glass marbles.

COLONIAL BRACKET LAMP

A piece of thin stock wrought iron wall plate is forged to the shape shown. Two lips are cut, drilled and bent out to serve as the swivel prongs for the bracket arm. Form the vertical plate for the bracket and join the horizontal and the twisted bracing arm to it. Use a long iron rivet pin to connect the arms with its vertical plate and to the swivel prongs. The front end of the bracket is forged flat and both pieces drilled together to accept a short nipple. Make an open harp whose three arms open on top to allow a lampshade to rest solidly on its forked prongs. Add a candle socket with the thumb twist switch extending below. The lamp shade, made

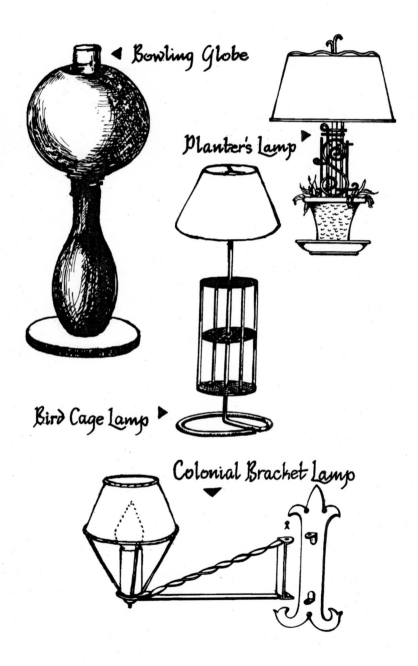

◄ Bowling Globe

Planter's Lamp ►

Bird Cage Lamp ►

Colonial Bracket Lamp
▼

of antiqued paper parchment has two heavy metal hoops framing it. The lamp cord is carried back along the bracket arm to accommodate itself to the swing.

TELESCOPING DESK LAMP

This lamp requires a wide, weighted base to maintain its stability no matter how the lamp is maneuvered. A long metal hood, somewhat resembling a section of roofing gutter is closed at both ends and attached to a flange arm on its center. Set in a single light 20 watt fluorescent unit with its push-button switch at the top, center of the lighthood. A long piece of frosted plastics with half-inch strips cemented inside in parallel rows to act as louvres is clip-hinged to the front edge of the reflector hood. These hinges should be tight so that they remain in position even if only partially open. A fifteen inch square tube is fastened to the base and joined at the top to a telescoping arm by a universal swivel joint. The telescoping extension resembles that type of collapsible camera tripod leg excepting that each section is no more than eight inches. The thin end uses an elbow joint to connect with the lamp unit of the structure. This may be made in polished metal or painted to suit the room harmony. The lamp base may be of marble or weighted wood.

COLONIAL BRACKET CLAMP-ON

This lamp is intended as an auxiliary piece to be clamped on to some end or occasional table. The upright is a wooden square along which the sliding bracket mechanism moves. The weight of the extension arm and lampshade throws the vertical alignment of the sliding arm off causing it to thrust inward and pinch clamp itself to the pole. The upper gripping arm simply slides down holding the bracket arm pin in place to permit it to swing. The fastening device on the bottom works in much the same way excepting that the side thrust is caused by the pressure exerted by the wooden thumb screw. A long nipple and swivel joint holds the lamp socket in place. The lamp shade grips the socket by its uno-bridge fitting. Cretonne or chintz makes an excellent combination with cherry or maple.

MOBILE—CANDELABRA

A metal, square tapered shank set upon an inverted metal plate is a fine body for this candelabra. This upper part of the shank is topped with a dual-socket attachment into each of which a fifteen inch polished, flex-cable, gooseneck is attached. On the free end of the gooseneck a cubed box is set. The extension arm enters one side, the thumb-turn switch extends from the bottom and a cup and candle socket is attached. The individual-sized lamp shade fits above the candle sleeve with a uno-bridge attachment fixed to the bottom hoop of the shade. All this enables one to bend the arms to many and varied positions either symmetrically or in occultly asymetric balance lending it a modern touch.

VANITY—CLUSTER LAMP

Attach two, shaped and rigid pipes to bottom of deep, metal and weighted bowl. Add a length of flexible gooseneck shaft to each with an outside coupling or bushing. The free end is connected to a metal bowl reflector with an oval harp under the lamp socket. Set a metal reflector plate on the harp screw, held down by a button finial. Fix a push button switch in the center of the base bowl, the lamp extension cord exiting from its side. Spray it with a soft-hued crackle color unless it must fit a specific decorative scheme. This lamp has the versatility of acting as a candelabrum, as a pair of lamps or as individual units serving different, though close-by areas.

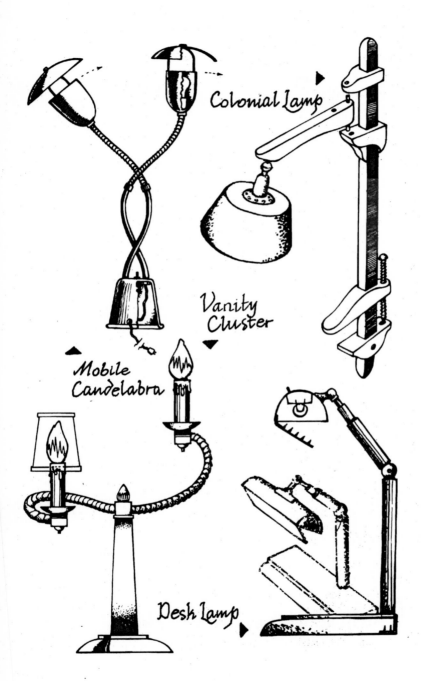

Colonial Lamp

Vanity Cluster

Mobile Candelabra

Desk Lamp

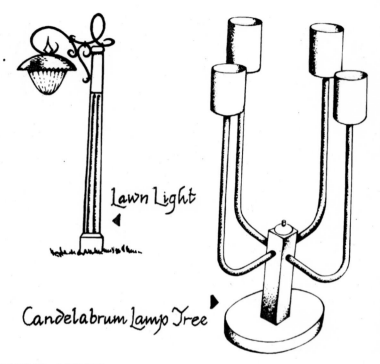

Lawn Light ◄

Candelabrum Lamp Tree ►

LAWN LIGHT

This is a private street lamp which has a wooden post built around the B-X cable which comes out of its ground outlet box extending up to the lamp at the top. The post may be reeded, fluted, or kept unadorned except for its base and cap piece. The wrought iron pieces should be shaped out of shallow "U" bar except where the B-X cable extends toward the lamp socket. There deeper "U" bars or even hollow square iron tubes might be used to hide the ungainly cable. The metal reflector shade acts as a weather protecting canopy for the socket section. The bottom glass globe is so fastened that it may be removed as needed without too much complication. Protect all exposed parts with outdoor paint to match the color scheme of its surroundings.

CANDELABRUM LAMP TREE

Four deep drum shades made of spun glass on wire frames clip on to the individual lamp bulbs of this candelabrum. The sockets tip four very long, vertical pipe arms which bend in on short, graceful 90° curves to be fastened to a center, metal tubular post. This, in turn, is brazed on to a large diametered circular disc with vertical sides. The top of this hollow post terminates with a cap in which a decorative push button switch is inserted. The length of the post and arms are optional and determined by the place in decoration it will occupy as is the wattage and size of the lamps. The metal frame may be of polished metal like brass, or aluminum or of conglomerate metals which are finally painted.

Conclusion

Glossary of Terms

A.C. CURRENT—An electrical charge which alternates its direction of flow at regular intervals.

ACETATE—General name for fabric made from cellulose acetate yarns such as Celanese, Acele, Seraceta, Rayon.

ACRYLATE RESIN—One of the group of acrylic resins in the glasslike thermoplasts like Lucite or Plexiglas.

AMINO PLASTIC—A synthetic resin (thermoset) made from the amino or amido compounds.

AMPERE—Is the measure of how many units (conlombs) of electricity that pass a given point within one second.

ANODIZING—A method of coloring and coating a metal with a protective film by subjecting it to an electrolytic action as the anodes of a cell.

APPLIQUE—Cut-out ornamentation applied or laid on another. The method of adherence depends upon the materials involved.

ARTIFICIAL LEATHER—Substitute for leather. Made of cotton cloth with plastic coating. Embossed and colored to imitate various leathers.

ASBESTOS—A fireproof and acid proof material of mineral origin. Long, straight, lustrous fibers spun and woven with cotton; later burned away. Difficult to spin; not dyed.

BAFFLES—A series of plates or screens set to cover a lamplight in order to deflect or regulate the light.

BALANCE—The state of equilibrium and counterforces achieved by the distribution of visual artistic elements.

BALLAST—A current-steadying device used with a fluorescent lamp.

BASKET CLOTH (Monk's cloth)—Is a plain-woven fabric with two or more warp threads used as a unit in its weaving.

BAS-RELIEF (Low Relief)—The projection of figures and ornamentation from the background to a degree lower than normal.

BATIK—Is a Javanese process of resist dyeing on cotton by painting or pouring molten wax in a design to keep it from being colored when the cloth is dip-dyed. The wax is removed afterward. This is imitated by machine printing.

BATTERY—A container of a limited reservoir of electrical charge.

BISCUIT FIRING—Is first heating of the clay adheres to the ceramic ware.

BLACK LIGHT—The light of the ultra-violet scale used to excite fluorescent or phosphorescent materials.

BLIND TOOLING—To shape, form or finish ornamentation on leather, etc., without use of gilding, inking or coloring.

BLOCK PRINTING—Is the decoration of fabrics by hand printing with carved wooden (sometimes linoleum, cork or rubber) blocks as distinguished from the modern printing with copper rollers.

BODY—A term used to designate center portion of a lighting fixture to which the arms and branches are attached.

BOOK CLOTH—Is a coarse plain-woven cloth heavily sized and embossed. Its very smooth surface makes easy application of painted or printed decoration.

BRAZING—To solder with a relatively infusible alloy such as brass or hard solder.

BRUSHES—Are parts of a motor which convey the voltage of a generator out of an outside line or into a motor from an outside source.

BULB—Is the bowl, usually glass, which encases the mechanism of the lamp.

CALENDERING—Adding a luster and smoothness to linen by passing it through steam rollers.

CANDLE—The paper cylinder sleeve which slips over the socket to simulate a candle.

CELLOPHANE—Is transparent sheeting of spent cellulose acetate which may be gotten in an array of colors.

CERAMICS—Is the art of making pottery.

CHASING—The method of ornamenting by grooving or indenting metal with an embossed or sculptured effect.

CHINA—Is a ceramic product which is non-porous, glazed and translucent.

CHINTZ—Originally referred to any printed cotton fabric, same as calico did, now is a small gay figured (sometimes large motif) fabric. Some chintzes have a glazed surface and are called "glazed chintz."

CELLULOSE RESINS—A group of synthetic thermoplastic materials containing cellulose as its basic chemical.

CIRCUIT—Is the path of flow taken by electrical current from its source to its piece of apparatus and back.

COATED FABRIC—A covering or lamination of smooth material on a fabric to give it luster, strength and new texture.

COLD LIGHT—Illumination which is accompanied by low heat, usually free of fluorescent light.

COLORFAST—Is the name applied to certain cotton fabrics whose color will not run when wetted or washed.

COMBINATION CIRCUIT—Is one in which there is both a parallel and a series circuit.

COMPOSITION—Is a substitute for wood, usually pressed in a mold to imitate carvings.

CONDUCTORS—Are those materials which offer little or no resistance to the flow of current.

CONFIGURED GLASS—A patterned or irregular surfacing of glass usually applied during its manufacture. It is not transparent and somewhat diffusing.

CORDUROY—Is derived from the French "corde du Roi" meaning King's cord, is a kind of cotton velvet having ridges or cords in the pile.

COULOMB—Is a unit which measures a definite quantity of electricity that passes a given point within one second.

COVE LIGHT—Illumination which originates in a trench-like strip and usually offers up indirect lighting to the area.

CRASH—Is the term applied to several rough fabrics having coarse uneven yarns and rough textures like crash linen or cotton.

CRAZING—Describes the condition of the surface which has cracked because of uneven cooling and shrinking.

CREPE—Is the general term covering many kinds of crinkled, puckering or unevened surface materials. There are many such effects such as rough, crinkle, flat or plissé crepes.

CRETONNE—Is a printed fabric of cotton or linen in all varieties of weaves and finishes, even chintz.

CRYSTAL—Short for rock-crystal, is a clear variety of quartz which looks like glass but is much harder.

CUT GLASS—Glass, usually flint, which is shaped or ornamented by cutting, grinding and polishing.

CURRENT—Of electricity is the measure (in amperes) of the quantity passing through a conductor in ONE SECOND.

DAMASCENING—The art of decorating metals by forging one metal into the hollowed areas of another metal in imitation of the steel decorating done in early Damascus.

D.C. CURRENT—An electrical charge which flows in one direction only.

DECALCOMANIA—Is a processed paper from which a design may be transferred to another surface.

DECORATED GLASS—A glass to whose surface some manner of decoration is applied.

DECOUPAGE—Paste-on of picture cut-outs upon objects to simulate an effect of inlay or marquetry work.

DIAPER DESIGN—A regular, all-over repeat of a diamond-shaped, trellised pattern.

DIMMER—Is a device used to regulate the flow of electricity. It is usually used to reduce or increase the efficiency of the lamp or apparatus not beyond one hundred per cent.

DIRECT LIGHT—Light which reaches its obective directly from its source of illumination.

DIRECT PRINTING—Is the method of printing cloth from engraved rolls or blocks much in the same way wallpaper is printed.

DISCHARGE PRINTING—Is the method of printing on dark materials after the fabric is piece-dyed. The color is removed or bleached from prescribed areas by chemicals to form light-toned units; sometimes called "extract" printing.

DOMINANCE—Achieving controlling attention within a unified group of compositional parts.

DRY CELL BATTERY—A voltaic (electric) cell whose contents has been treated by use of some absorbent carrier to insure its not spilling.

DRYPOINT—A method of engraving with a needle instead of a burin or with acid.

DYEING—Is the process of coloring materials. Variations of this are cross-dyeing, dip-dyeing, ingrain-dyeing, piece-dyeing, stock dyeing or yarn-dyeing.

DYNAMO—Is a term used to include both a motor and a generator. It may be used as either depending upon whether it is being fed mechanical or electrical power. It will deliver the opposite type of energy.

EFFICIENCY—Is the percentage of power delivered by a machine against the power used to supply this same machine. It can never equal 100, it is always less.

ELECTRICITY—Is the flow of current along a conductor.

ELECTROLYTE—A substance in which the conduction of electricity is accomplished by chemical decomposition.

ELECTRODE—Either terminal by which an electric current enters or leaves an electric body source (electrolyte).

EMBOSSING—Is the texture of raised effect gotten by pressing the fabric or leather between engraved rollers with the aid of heat.

ENAMELING—Applying a vitreous composition for coating the surface of metal.

ENERGY and WORK—Is the mechanical energy measured in terms of horsepower X the hours in which it is used.

ENGRAVING—An incising method of producing decorations on wood, metal, stone, etc.

ETCHING—The art of producing designs by means of "biting" into metal with an acid.

EXTENSION CORD—A length of electric wire needed to reach a nearby outlet often used on a portable item.

FABRIC—Is cloth, goods or textile material woven or knitted of any textile fibers.

FELT—Cloth formed by the action of heat, moisture, and friction on wool fibers.

FILAMENT—Is a single strand of fiber or metal used in weaving or as an electric conductor-resistor to bring on incandescence.

FILTERS—A special screen used to partially absorb or change the character of light rays.

FINIAL—The terminal knob or ornament usually the nut which fastens the shade washer to the harp screw or the lowest ornament of the chandelier types.

FINISHING—Refers to all processes after the construction or assemblage process have been completed.

FLOCKING—Is the process of applying designs or covering on materials by blowing on ground flocks (fibers of wool, spun glass, asbestos or other fibers) over a surface previously printed, sprayed or painted with an adherent.

FLUORESCENT—A type of illumination which depends upon a substance which when stimulated gives off light.

FLUTING—Is the decoration achieved by means of parallel channels or flutes.

FLUX—A material used in soldering to prevent the metals from oxidizing during the heating process.

FREQUENCY OF CURRENT—The number of alternations or directional changes of the A.C. current per second.

FRET—Is the ornamental work of an interlaced design, either pierced or a solid background.

FROSTED GLASS—A glass whose surface, one or both, have been roughened to increase the diffusion of the light.

FUR—Is the hair-covered skin of an animal.

FUR FABRICS—Are the large class of pile fabrics which are made to imitate fur.

FUSE—Is a protective device in an electric circuit, usually a conductor which melts, thus breaking the circuit at a preset danger point.

GAUGE—A measure of thickness standards within specified limits and usually applied to metals and wires.

GENERAL LIGHT—Light designed to cover the entire area with an even amount of illumination.

GENERATORS—Are machines designed to transform mechanical power into electricity.

GILDING—A superficial coating of gold or covering it with some material to give it a golden coloring.

GINGHAM—Is a yarn-dyed fabric woven in checks, plaids, stripes or plain colors.

GLAZE—Is a mixture of feldspar and other ingredients, which is used to cover the surface of the pottery.

GLASS—A clear transparent material made up principally of silica, potash, lime and other incidental elements. Referred to as clear, crystal, flint.

GOOSENECK—A curved pipe form, sometimes flexible, sometimes rigid.

GRAIN—The term used to indicate the outer or hair side of the hide or skin when it is split into more than two thicknesses. It is the direction of the long fibers of lumber.

GRAY CARVING—Grinding ornamentation on the reverse side of glass to be viewed from the front. These surfaces are left gray-unpolished.

GROSGRAIN—Meaning "coarse grain" is a firm, stiff, closely woven corded fabric.

GROUND—Is the connection made in grounding a circuit.

HARDWOOD—Is the lumber gotten from a tree whose cell walls are thicker and more tightly packed.

HIGH RELIEF—The projection of ornamentation from its background for half or more than half of its natural circumference.

HOMESPUN—Is a loose, rough fabric made of coarse woolen fibers. It is similar to tweed in general character.

HORSE POWER—A unit of power equal to 550 foot-pounds of work per second, the power which a horse exerts in pulling, equal to ¾ of a kilowatt or 750 watts.

HUE—The quality of a color which identifies it as red, blue, green, yellow, etc.

IGNEOUS ROCK—Rock originally formed by hot, molten lavas—affectionately known as fire rocklike granite.

IMPREGNATED CLOTH—Cloth permeated or saturated with another material to add new desirable properties.

INCANDESCENT—Light which is derived from a filament made luminous by heat.

INDIRECT LIGHT—Light which reaches its objective in an indirect route from its source as from an intervening reflecting surface.

INFRA-RED—The color whose long wave-length is just below the line of visibility. It is within the area of heat generation.

INSULATORS—Are those materials which offer almost total resistance to the flow of current.

INTAGLIO—Incising ornamentation below the surface of the material so that an impression of relief imagery is gotten.

INTENSITY—The point of saturation of pure hue contained in a color, sometimes referred to as chroma.

JACQUARD—Is the technique of reproducing complicated pictures on all cloths using the Jacquard loom to do so.

JASPE—Meaning streaked or striped is a faint, broken striped effect, usually woven from printed yarns.

KAPOK—Is the trade name for a colorfast fabric made of artificial silk.

KEENE CEMENT—A form of spent plaster ot paris which results in a harder material, once cast.

KEYLESS—A fixture which has no switch on the unit itself.

KEY LIGHT—The average degree of general illumination such as high or low.

KILOWATT—Equals 1000 watts (1⅓) horsepower.

KILOWATT HOURS—Is the commercial measure of kilowatts used X hours during which it is used.

LAMINATION—The process of bonding together superimposed layers of paper, wood, fabric, resinoid on a body material.

LAMP—The mechanism which creates the illuminating waves. It is sometimes used to designate the entire fixture used with the lamp.

LAPIDARY—The art of cutting or engraving upon stone, precious or otherwise.

LENS—A kind of transparent substance used to change the direction of rays of light to form an image within a particular focus.

LINE DROP—Is the loss of voltage which is used in forcing the current through the wire toward its destination. The greater the distance, the greater is the line drop.

LISLE FINISH—Is a process by which the short, projecting fibers are removed from fine-grade cotton yarns by running them over gas flames.

LOADING or WEIGHTING—Is the addition of any substance to increase the weight of a fabric.

LOUVRES—A slatted arrangement of panels to permit openings for light or ventilation.

LUSTERING—Is a finishing process which produces a luster on cloth by means of heat and pressure.

MARQUETRY—A method of decorating wood with small pieces of cut-outs matched like a jig-saw puzzle to cover the surface.

MERCERIZING—Cotton fabrics or fibers treated with caustic alkali making it more receptive to dyes, often making it silkier.

METALLIC CLOTH—Is a decorative fabric used mainly for trimming and made of metal filling with cotton warp. These filling yarns are produced by winding a strip of tinsel around cotton yarn.

METAMORPHIC ROCK—Igneous or sedimentary rock which has been altered by heat, pressure or chemical action like marble.

MICA—One of the mineral silicates which readily separate into very thin sheets. The transparent form is commonly called isinglass.

MINUS—(—) Is the point toward which electrical current will flow. (Cathode.)

MODELING—A technique of shaping materials by pressing or molding it as with a soft material.

MOGUL SOCKET—A socket of larger diameter usually used with commercial lamps.

MOIRE—Meaning "watered" is a finish on silk, cotton, rayon or other plain weave fabrics which are often corded. This is done by engraved rollers passing over the surface, flattening it with heat and pressure and at intervals leaving the natural roundness in contrast.

MOTIF—Is the controlling idea or leading feature of a design.

MOTORS—Are machines made to convert electrical power into mechanical power.

MULTIPLE CIRCUIT—Is another name for a parallel circuit.

MUSLIN—Named after the ancient city of Mosul where it was first made; is a firm, plain white strong heavy cotton fabric.

NAP—Unlike pile, is the fuzzy appearance produced by raising the fibers of the cloth as in flannel.

NET—Is a mesh-weave cloth which may leave a variety of shaped openings.

NOVELTY FABRICS—Cover the large class of materials made to meet a style demand or special need. They have not become staple.

NYLON PLASTICS—A synthetic material derived from coal, air and water which can be produced in many forms like thread, sheets, etc.

OHMS—Are the units of "friction" (resistance) measured which a conductor offers to a current. Some conductors offer more, some less. Hence they are called poor or good electrical conductors.

OPAL GLASS—A white or milky-white glass with a high light diffusing property.

OPAQUE—A surface or material impervious to light.

OUTLET—An electrical fitting at which the wires terminate for further connection.

OVERLOAD—Is an excessive load beyond the regular limit load of line or a piece of apparatus.

PAINTED FABRICS—Are colored free-hand in individual or exclusive pattern or picture.

PARALLEL CIRCUIT—Is that course which electricity must flow when pieces of electrical apparatus are connected side by side.

PATINA—A film or coloring formed on metal by age, exposure or chemical treatment.

PARCHMENT—An animal skin, formerly only of sheepskin, now substitute by others.

PHENOLIC PLASTIC—One of the thermosetting resins gotten by reaction of phenol with an aldehyde.

PIERCING—The process of perforating and removing parts of the material to create a design.

PILE—Is the surface of fabric made of upright ends resembling fur.

PLAID—Is a box-shaped design usually woven of dyed yarn though sometimes printed afterward.

PLAIN WEAVE—Is the simplest of the fundamental weaves often called "tabby" weave.

PLASTER OF PARIS—Powdered gypsum rock which when mixed with water forms a plastic mass that hardens.

PLATING—A thin coating of metal over some material usually applied by an electrical process.

PLUG—A pronged fitting for making an electrical connection by inserting it into a receptacle.

PLUS (+)—Is the point from which current flows—plus to minus. (Anode.)

POLKA DOT—Is an all-over pattern of round surface dots of any size embroidered, printed or flocked on to the surface of a fabric.

PYROGRAPHY—The art of producing pictures or designs on wood, leather or other such material by burning with hot instruments.

PORCELAIN—Is another term for China.

POTTERY—Is the resultant articles composed of clay and hardened by heat.

POWER (in watts)—Used up by any part of a circuit—the product of the current which flows through THAT PART of the circuit X the voltage in JUST THAT SAME PART of the circuit.

PRESSURE—Is that factor which causes to flow and not remain static.

PRINT—Is the general term referring to printed cotton fabrics. Cretonne, chintz and grandmother cloth are often called "prints."

PUNCHING—To perforate a mark or design by striking the material with a sharp tool so imprinted.

QUARTZ—A mineral, usually a variety of silicon oxide, which is crystalline in appearance when pure and often used for gems as is amethyst or for larger pieces made of rock-crystal.

RAMIE—Sometimes called "China grass," is a fabric made of the fibers of Oriental plant stalks which resemble flax.

RAYON—Is a fabric made of cellulose fibers converted from wood pulp or cotton linters which will vary in its properties depending upon the process used to make it.

REPOUSSE—Ornamentation formed in relief from the reverse side.

RHYTHM—The smoothness of eye-movement or attention offered by the parts of a design to create the gracefulness of the whole.

RIB—Is a ridge or cord effect in woven fabric made by heavy filling yarn.

RIVETING—The process of uniting two or more pieces by passing a shank through a hole in each piece then pressing or beating down the plain end to make a second head.

SANFORIZING—Is a pat nted process that prevents the shrinkage of washable fabrics.

SATIN—Is the name of a basic weave which looks like a broken twill. It usually has a high glossy finish.

SCONCE—A type of wall bracket consisting of one or more candlesticks.

SEDIMENTARY ROCK—Rock laid down by water, wind or results of organic deposits like limestone or sandstone.

SELVEDGE or SELVAGE—Is the finished edge on a woven or knitted fabric.

SERIES CIRCUIT—Is the course through which electricity must pass when pieces of electrical apparatus are connected in tandem.

SHADOW or WARP PRINT—Is the faint or shadowy design gotten by printing it on the warp and weaving over it with plain filling. It is reversible.

SHORT CIRCUIT—A circuit usually made through a part having a lower resistance than the rest and resulting in burning out the circuit fuse.

SHUNT—Is the means used to supply another path for an electrical current.

SILK SCREEN—Imprinting designs on materials by means of using silk as a stencil.

SIZING—Is a finishing process in which yarn and cloth are treated with stiffening substances to give strength, stiffness and smoothness to it.

SKIVED—To shave or pare leather on the reverse side causing it to become thinner.

SOCKET—The part of the fixture which serves as the holder for the electrical connection.

SOFTWOOD—Is applied to lumber made from trees which have thin cells and more uniform in size.

SOLDERING—The method of joining metallic surfaces using an alloy which melts readily at low temperatures.

SPECIFIC LIGHT—Light designed to reach and illuminate a definite area in a room.

SPECTRUM—The visible range of colors extending from the shortest to the longest wave length. Its best known example is the rainbow.

SPLICE—A joining or junction of wires according to safety regulations.

SPOTLIGHT—A concentrated area of illumination to such high key that it is accented against its surroundings.

STAMPING—To forcibly impress or indent a mark or decoration with a stamp, a cut or a die.

STENCIL—A method of making reproductions of pictures, etc., by means of blocking off designated areas with a mask and forcing pigment through the pierced areas.

STORAGE BATTERY—A series of connected electro-chemical cells used to generate electrical energy. May be recharged by reversing the direction of the flow of current.

STYRENE PLASTICS—A plastic material of the unsaturated hydrocarbon family (cinnamic acid) used to make polystyrene plastic (thermoplast).

SWITCH—A device used to control the flow of electricity into the fixture.

TANNING—Process of preparing a skin and making leather out of it.

TAPA CLOTH—Is made without spinning or weaving. It is made by beating flat the inner bark of certain tropical trees in the South Sea Islands to resemble cloth. Usually decorated with batik prints.

TERMINALS—Are the points to and from which current passes through a piece of electrical apparatus.

TEXTURE—Is the surface effect.

THERMOPLAST—A synthetic resinoid material which has the property of becoming soft under application of heat and rigid at normal temperatures no matter how often it is repeated.

THERMOSET—A synthetic resin which has the property of becoming permanently rigid by applying heat which affects a chemical change.

TIE DYE—Is a hand method of producing patterns on cloth when it is dipped in a dye-bath after portions of it has been tied or knotted firmly to create dye-resist areas.

TINNED—To cover a metal with a thin coat of soft solder in preparation for a permanent joint.

TINSEL—Is a synthetic metal filament wound around cotton or silk yarn and used in metal cloth or brocades in imitation of the historic "cloth of gold."

TOILE de JOUY—Is a pictorial print on cotton, usually one color on a light ground, after the manner of the 18th and early 19th Century French prints made at Jouy.

TONE (Value)—The white and black modification of a color. The dark or light quality inherent in a color.

TRANSFORMER—An apparatus used to change electric current from high to low (step-down) or from low to high (step-up) without changing the current energy. Sometimes used interchangeably with a converter.

TWILL—Is a fundamental weave usually recognized by its formed lines running diagonally.

ULTRA-VIOLET—The range of colors beyond the visible short-wave-lengths at the violet end.

UNDERWRITERS' CODE—A set of standards decided on by the union of Insurance Companies which are the minimum requirements for safety.

UNION—Is the term applied to fabrics which combine cotton warp with linen filling or cotton with wool filling.

VELLUM—A fine grade of translucent goatskin, resembling parchment.

VENEER—A thin layer of special material overlayed on some kind of a cove to improve it.

VINYL RESIN PLASTIC—A synthetic material of the thermoplastic group formed by the polymerizing of a vinyl compound.

VOLTAGE—Is the measure of pressure against resistance across two points in a line. It is the product of the amperes X the ohms (unit of resistance measure) or watts divided by amperes.

WARP—Is the set of yarn or threads which runs lengthwise in a piece of woven cloth.

WATT—Is a small unit of electric power; power in watts = volts X amperes.

WAVE LENGTH—The distance between corresponding points on any two consecutive electric waves.

WEAVE—Is to interlace warp threads with filling yarn to form cloth.

WEFT—Is another term for filling or woof.

WEIGHTED SILK—Is gotten when metallic salts are added to the silk.

WELDING—The process of uniting metallic parts by heating the surfaces of the joining parts until melted and allowing the metals to flow together then cool to hardness.

WIRING—To connect the various parts of an electrical circuit with wire conductors.

WOOF—See Weft.

YARN—Is a continuous strand of spun fiber used for weaving or knitting. Used interchangeably with thread although thread is used for sewing and not weaving.

Lightning Source UK Ltd.
Milton Keynes UK
UKOW03f0014221013

219514UK00001B/139/P